Mustangs

By Lorrine Gillespie

Reading Consultant:

Scott M. Moen

Wisconsin Early Mustangers

C A P S T O N E   P R E S S

M A N K A T O ,   M I N N E S O T A

C A P S T O N E   P R E S S
818 North Willow Street • Mankato, MN 56001

Library of Congress Cataloging-in-Publication Data
Gillespie, Lorrine.
    Mustangs/by Lorrine Gillespie.
    p. cm. -- (High performance)
    Includes bibliographical references and index.
    Summary: Gives an overview of the history of the classic Ford sports car,
the Mustang, describing some notable models.
    ISBN 1-56065-392-2
    1. Mustang automobile--Juvenile literature. [1. Mustang automobile--
History.] I. Title. II. Series: High performance (Mankato, Minn.)
TL215.M8G52 1996
629.222'2--dc20

96-47765
CIP
AC

Photo credits
Behring Automobile Musem, 30. Ford Motor Company, 12,
34-38. FPG, 11, 28; Mark Beinstein, 6, 32; Dave Gettlen, 8;
Michael Kornafel, 18; Buddy Mays, 4; Robert Reiff, 14, 20,
22; Dean Siracusa, 10. Stokka Productions, cover.
Unicorn/Wayne Floyd, 13; Rod Furgason, 25; Jeff Greenberg,
17, 42; Arni Katz, 19. Visuals Unlimited/Jeff Greenberg, 26,
40.

Table of Contents

Words in **boldface** type in the text are defined
in the Glossary in the back of this book.

Chapter 1

The Pony Car

The Mustang is a four-seated sports car. It is named after wild horses living in the Southwest United States. The wild horses are called Mustangs, too. The Mustang sports car is made by the Ford Motor Company. It is one of the greatest success stories in the automobile industry.

Many people call Mustangs pony cars. An **insignia** of the wild horse is on the Mustang's **grille**. The insignia reminds people that the car is as spirited as the wild horse it is named after.

The Mustang sports car is named after wild horses.

Chapter 2

Birth of the Mustang

European sports cars became popular in the early 1960s. Some of the best-selling models were made by Triumph, MG, and Austin Healey.

North American carmakers tried to compete with the Europeans. General Motors was one of these North American carmakers. General Motors' top sports car was the Corvette. It was the most popular North American sports car of the time.

Ford wanted to develop a car that would compete, too. Ford chose a talented executive to lead the design team. That executive was Lee Iacocca (eye-uh-COKE-uh).

Lee Iacocca led the team that designed the Mustang.

Lee Iacocca

Iacocca is the son of Italian immigrants. He started working at the Ford Motor Company in 1946. He was 22 years old.

Iacocca started as an engineer at Ford. But he soon showed a talent for selling cars. His selling ability led to many promotions. Iacocca became Ford's general manager in 1960.

Guiding the plans for a new sports car was a huge responsibility. Iacocca wanted the new car to be as popular as the European sports cars. He wanted it to be as popular as the Corvette.

Iacocca put together a team of men and women with youthful ideas. They were called the Fairlane Committee. The committee's task was to come up with a small, light, affordable sports car.

Iacocca wanted the Mustang to be as popular as the Corvette, which was General Motors' top sports car.

Secret Meetings

The Fairlane Committee was named after the Fairlane Motel in Dearborn, Michigan, where it met. The meetings were secret.

The committee worked long hours. Iacocca did not want anyone else to know what the committee members were doing. He burned all their notes, and any other paper they wrote on. That way no one could dig through the trash to learn about the committee's work.

The public first saw the Mustang in 1964.

People fell in love with the Mustang.

The First Sighting

On March 11, 1964, Henry Ford II's nephew drove a pre-production Mustang convertible to a luncheon in downtown Detroit. Pictures of the Mustang showed up in newspapers and on television the next day.

The photos were grainy. They looked like spy photos. Many car lovers who saw the

Working-class people could afford the new Mustang.

photos were curious about Ford's new sports car.

The World's Fair

The Mustang was officially shown to the public on April 17, 1964, at the New York World's Fair. The new Mustang looked and drove like a European sports car. It cost half the price, though. Millions of working-class people could afford one.

People went crazy over the Mustang. Ford had not had a car as popular since the **Model T**. One million Mustangs were sold between April 1964 and August 1965. It was a new record.

The Mustang broke sales records that had been standing since the time of the Model T.

Chapter 3

The First Mustangs

Ford built the first Mustangs in three different styles. The styles were called faces. Ford called them the three faces of Mustang.

One of the faces was the affordable Mustang. Another face was the luxury Mustang. A third face was the sporty Mustang. By building three models, Ford tried to make everyone a buyer.

The Affordable Mustang

The affordable Mustang was designed to appeal to the average car buyer. It looked nice. It did not cost too much. It had wall-to-wall

The affordable Mustang appealed to the average buyer.

carpeting, bucket seats, and a sporty steering wheel.

Many people wanted the affordable car. Ford had to build new plants to fill all the orders.

The Luxury Mustang

Buyers could change the Mustang's appearance. People who wanted a luxury Mustang could pick their own package of options.

A **V-8** engine was one of the options. Buyers could choose from three different **transmissions**. Power steering was another option. An AM radio with push buttons was an option. Many buyers added pinstripes and air conditioning.

The most prized option was the deluxe interior. The deluxe interior had five dials on the instrument panel. It had a steering wheel that looked like it was made of wood. A herd of running horses was **embossed** on the seats.

Every Mustang had a sporty-looking interior.

Cars with deluxe interiors are now rare. They are collectibles.

The Sporty Mustang

The third style was the sporty Mustang. It had a long hood and a **fastback**. Even the interior was sporty. It had bucket seats and a stylish instrument panel.

The sporty look is what made the Mustang famous. No other car looked like it. Iacocca's dreams for the Mustang had come true.

The sporty Mustang had a fastback.

Shelby's Cobras were speedsters at the racetrack.

Shelby Mustangs

The people at Ford wanted to make a racing Mustang, too. Iacocca called a man named Carroll Shelby. Shelby was a successful race-car driver.

Shelby had made his own sports car in the early 1960s. It was called the Cobra. It was powered by a Ford engine. Shelby's Cobras were blowing Corvettes off the racetrack.

Iacocca shipped 100 white Mustangs to Shelby's plant in California. They were fastbacks. They had high-performance, 289-cubic-inch (4,740 cubic-centimeter) engines.

Shelby turned the cars into racers. He redesigned the body. The Shelby engine had 306 **horsepower**. The car could go 125 miles (200 kilometers) per hour. Shelby's cars were approved for the 1965 racing season.

The Muscle Tradition

Shelby made many different Cobras and Mustangs for Ford. These were limited **production cars**. This means not very many were made. The engines and body styles changed every year. They changed to stay ahead of the competition.

Shelby's cars were the first Ford muscle cars. Muscle cars are made to perform like race cars yet be driven on regular roads. They accelerate quickly, reaching high speeds.

Shelby's Mustangs and Cobras were Ford's first muscle cars.

Chapter 4

The Performance Generation

Mustangs built from 1969 to 1973 are high performance Mustangs. The high performance cars were faster than the first Mustangs. These were muscle cars. The engines were bigger. They could reach high speeds quickly. Some of their names were Mach 1, Boss, and Cobra Jet.

1969/1970 GT 350 and GT 500

The 1969/1970 GT 350 and GT 500 were the last Mustangs Shelby made for Ford. They were available as either **fastbacks** or convertibles. The GT 500 had a bigger engine than the GT 350. Otherwise, they were the same car.

The GT 350 was one of the last Shelby Mustangs.

The GT 350's engine was called the 351 Windsor. The GT 500's engine was called the 428 Cobra Jet. The Cobra Jet was one of the biggest and best muscle car engines. Many people say it was the fastest muscle-car engine ever.

These GTs mixed high performance with high styling. They had fiberglass fenders and hoods. The fiberglass hoods had five **air ducts**. There were more air ducts on the front fenders. There were fiberglass **scoops** on the rear fenders. These helped cool the back brakes.

The Boss 429

Ford made the 429-cubic-inch (7,036-cubic-centimeter) engine for its race cars. Racing rules said that 500 of the engines had to be sold in production cars. Ford had to sell the 429 to the public.

Originally, the 429 engine was going to go into the Ford Talledega and Ford Cyclone Spoiler. But the engine was not ready at the time the cars were built. Ford had to put the 429 into a different car.

Mustangs built from 1969 to 1973 were muscle cars.

Ford decided to put the engines in the
Mustang. The 429 engines went into cars that
were supposed to get the 428 Cobra Jet.
Engineers had to squeeze the huge 429 into a
space designed for a much smaller engine.

The 429 was the biggest engine ever used in
a Mustang. It was called the Boss 429. Ford
made the Boss 429 in 1969 and 1970. Fewer
than 1,500 were made.

The Boss 302

The 302-cubic-inch (4,953 cubic-
centimeter) Boss engine was originally used in

The bigger Mustangs of the 1970s used a lot of gas.

race cars, too. It was designed to compete against the Chevy Camaro Z 28. The competition spread to the showroom in 1969. That was when the Boss 302 became a production car.

The Boss 302 was a high-revving engine. It was also the most efficient Ford muscle-car engine. From the factory, it was rated at 290 horsepower. Independent tests were done when the car was released. These tests showed that the Boss 302 actually produced 302 horsepower.

About 1,700 Boss 302s were made during the first year. Just over 7,000 were made in 1970. Boss Mustangs were probably the most popular Ford muscle cars ever built. Boss Mustangs are the only Mustangs with engine numbers and frame numbers that match.

Fuel Economy

In the early 1970s, many people became concerned about the supply of fuel. The Organization of Petroleum Exporting Countries (OPEC) raised the cost of oil. The price of gas went up. This created an **energy crisis**.

As gas prices went up, people wanted their cars to go as many miles as possible on a tank of gas. Fewer buyers wanted their cars to be big and fast.

The Mustang had grown eight inches (20 centimeters) longer by 1971. It had grown six inches (15 centimeters) wider. It weighed 600 pounds (270 kilograms) more than the year before.

These bigger Mustangs used a lot of gas. Their price went up, too. The Mustang lost buyers who wanted affordable cars. Sales dropped 20 percent in the early 1970s.

Chapter 5
Mustang II

In 1974, Lee Iacocca guided the Mustang's redesign. Iacocca wanted the Mustang II to appeal to young drivers. It was built by a team of young designers. The design team wanted the new Mustang to look like a muscle car yet still be economical.

Ford called the new design the Mustang II. It began the second generation of Mustangs. It was light. It drove more miles per gallon of gas than the first-generation Mustangs.

The Mustang II came with either a four-**cylinder** or a six-cylinder engine. Ford stopped making Mustangs with V-8 engines.

New Advertising

Ford executives wanted to appeal to new customers. They studied the market. They

Iacocca guided the Mustang's redesign.

Ford introduced the Cobra II in 1976.

learned that more women had full-time jobs outside the home. They learned that women's salaries were increasing.

Ford featured young businesswomen in its ads. The ads worked. The Mustang II widened its appeal. Ford sold nearly half a million Mustang IIs in the first year.

The 1974 Mustang II was 20 inches (51 centimeters) shorter than the 1973 Mustang. It was 500 pounds (225 kilograms) lighter. The four-cylinder engine was the first North American engine based on metric dimensions.

The Cobra II and the Stallion

Ford brought back the V-8 Mustang in 1975. Ford introduced the Cobra II in 1976 with the

30

optional V-8. It looked something like the Shelby Cobras of the 1960s. The Cobra II had a rear **spoiler**, a fake hood scoop, and snake decals. It accelerated to 60 miles (96 kilometers) per hour in nine seconds.

Another Mustang model of the 1970s was called the Stallion. The Stallion was made in flashy colors. It could be ordered in bright red, bright yellow, silver-blue glow, and silver metallic.

The Ghia

In the mid 1970s, Ford bought an Italian car company called Ghia. Ford used the Ghia name to sell the luxury-model Mustang II. The designers at Ghia sent Ford plans just 53 days after they joined the Ford team.

The Ghia was first offered in 1974. It was available only as a two-door hardtop. It was an elegant car. The luxury package had Deluxe Fabric **Upholstery**, and a half vinyl top.

Ford sold nearly 200,000 Mustang IIs in 1978. Of those, nearly 35,000 were Ghias. The Mustang II showed that the pony car was not going away.

Chapter 6

New Generations

June 1978 was Ford's biggest sales month ever. Lee Iacocca had been with Ford for 32 years. He had been its president since 1970.

After a dispute with Henry Ford II in 1978, Iacocca left the Ford Motor Company. He became the president of the Chrysler Corporation. Chrysler was another North American carmaker.

But the Mustang went on without Iacocca. It had been around for nearly 15 years. It was a proven winner.

The Mustang's strongest competition continued to come from General Motors cars. At General Motors, the Pontiac Firebird and the Chevrolet Camaro had joined the Corvette as arch rivals of the Mustang.

Iacocca left Ford in 1978. He became Chrysler's president.

New Mustangs have kept the markings of the classic Mustangs.

The SVO

Ford introduced the SVO Mustang in the 1980s. SVO stands for Special Vehicle Operation. The SVO was a new breed of muscle car.

The SVO had a turbocharged four-cylinder engine. It could reach 60 miles (96 kilometers) per hour in less than 10 seconds. Camaros and Firebirds could not keep up with the SVO.

The Newest Breeds

New Mustangs have kept the markings of the classic Mustangs. They still have long hoods and short trunks. They still have three vertical stripes in the taillights. They still have the C-shaped scoop on the side panels. All of these features are Mustang **trademarks**.

The GT and the Cobra

Ford is still building fast Mustangs. Mustangs continue to beat Firebirds and Camaros on the test tracks. Today's Mustang buyers can choose from the standard Mustang, the Mustang GT, and the Mustang Cobra.

Ford is still building beautiful Mustangs.

The 1996 Cobra has a 32-valve V-8 engine.

The GT has a high-output V-8 engine. The instrument panel looks like the cockpit of a fighter jet. It has 16-inch speed-rated tires. Speed-rated tires are made to go faster than regular tires. Speed-rated tires are safer at high speeds.

The Cobra has a 32-valve V-8 engine with 305 horsepower. It reaches 60 miles (96 kilometers) per hour in five and one-half seconds. The Cobra speeds through the quarter-mile in 14 seconds. It received a superior rating in road-handling ability at 80 miles (128 kilometers) per hour on the test track.

Today's Mustang buyers can still get convertibles.

Chapter 7
Modern Safety

Ford has spent millions of dollars on safety research. Mustangs are safer than they have ever been. They will continue to become safer into the future.

Designers have tested the Mustang's frame. They have tested the surface of the car. Drivers have spent hours in Mustangs on the test track. They have tested the car's steering and handling.

Designers and drivers look for problems that might cause accidents. They do their testing on **pre-production cars**. If they find any problems, they fix them before they build cars to sell to the public.

Drivers have spent many hours in Mustangs on the test track.

Early Mustangs had lap belts only.

Seat Belts and Air Bags

In early Mustangs, lap belts in the front seats were the best safety feature. Later models added shoulder straps in front. Lap belts are now available for every passenger.

Air bags are one of the best safety features in new cars. Air bags expand at the time of an accident. Every Mustang produced today has two airbags. One is packed into the steering wheel. The other one is packed into the dashboard. They protect both the driver and the front-seat passenger.

In the future, air bags will be put inside the cars' door panels. These will protect the driver and any passengers in case of side collisions.

Intrusion Beams and Anti-Lock Brakes

New Mustang door panels have intrusion beams. The intrusion beam is a strong bar that reinforces the door. A reinforced door will not collapse very easily in an accident.

The Mustang GT has an anti-lock braking system. This system is known as ABS. Brakes on cars without ABS can lock up when the driver tries to stop the car in a hurry. Then the car can skid out of control.

ABS brakes are controlled by a computer. ABS brakes never lock the wheels. Cars with ABS brakes never skid out of control.

The Future

Mustangs will continue to be safe, affordable, luxurious, and sporty. There will be new designs. The new designs will be based on the classic Mustang look. It is a look that has proven itself.

The 1966 420 SC Cobra

Glossary

air ducts—openings in the body of a car through which air passes

cylinder—can-shaped areas of an engine that contain the pistons; where fuel is ignited

embossed—to raise a design above the surface

energy crisis—a period during the 1970s when the shortage of natural resources was widely realized, and oil prices skyrocketed

fastback—a type of car body with a sloping roof

grille—the bars or fins in front of a car or truck's radiator, between the headlights

horsepower—a unit used to measure the power of engines and motors

insignia—an ornament, badge, or other special mark of honor

Model T—the first popular car designed on Henry Ford's assembly line; more than 15 million were sold

pre-production cars—cars built for testing purposes before the model is mass produced

production cars—cars built for sale to the public

scoops—large air ducts

spoiler—part of a car, usually a long, rigid flap, that breaks the air flow to make a car handle better

trademark—a design or feature used by a manufacturer to distinguish a product

transmission—gears that transfer power from the engine to the wheels

upholstery—fabric covering much of a car's interior

V-8—an engine with eight cylinders set in pairs at angles forming the shape of the letter V

To Learn More

Knudson, Richard L. *Restoring Yesterday's Cars*. Minneapolis: Lerner, 1982.

Ready, Kirk L. *Custom Cars*. Minneapolis: Lerner, 1982

Royston, Angela. *Cars*. New York: Aladdin Books, 1991.

Witzenburg, Gary L. *Mustang! The Complete History of America's Pioneer Pony Car*. Princeton, N.J.: Automobile Quarterly, 1979.

Useful Addresses

Club Mustang Quebec
512 Bois-Joli
Ste-Marie de Beauce, PQ G6E 3B9
Canada

Mustang Club of America
P.O. Box 447
Lithonia, GA 30058-0447

Mustang Monthly
3816 Industry Boulevard
Lakeland, FL 33811

Mustang Owners Club of America
2720 Tennessee NE
Albuquerque, NM 87710

Internet Sites

Classic Mustang Page
http://www.dwx.com/~bob/topics/mustang

Late Model Mustang Page
http://www.onetinc.com/~hectorn

Mustangs and Fabulous Fords
ftp://cadiris.indstate.edu/mustang.html

Index